Curious Avenue

by Tom Toles

Andrews and McMeel
A Universal Press Syndicate Company
Kansas City

For Amanda and Seth

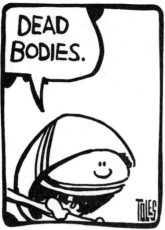

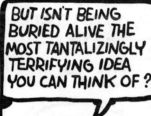

IT'S DEFINITELY BEST WHEN BOTH MOM AND DAD ARE HOME.

I CAN PLAY FOR A WHILE NEAR DAD...

...THEN WANDER OVER AND SPEND SOME TIME WITH MOM.

BACK AND FORTH. BACK AND FORTH.

UNTIL MY MOM THINKS DAD IS WATCHING ME AND MY DAD THINKS MOM IS WATCHING ME.

THEN I CAN WANDER OFF AND PLAY WITH THE DANGEROUS TOOLS IN MILLER'S GARAGE.

25

VIOLET, CAN I BORROW YOUR "WEAKLY NOOZ"?

THE ONE WITH THE STORY ABOUT THE HEAD BEING KEPT ALIVE IN A GALVANIZED PAIL.

THANKS. IT'S THE "NEWSPAPER FOR LIVELY MINDS" LIKE MINE.

WANT TO ALSO BORROW A GALVANIZED PAIL?

SONNY, LISTEN TO THIS STORY: "WOMAN GIVES BIRTH TO OWN GRANDPARENTS."

WHERE DO THEY GET STORIES LIKE THAT?

THEY MAKE THEM UP.

LET'S START A NEWSPAPER!

WE'LL CALL OUR NEWSPAPER "THE CURIOUS OBSERVER."

HELP ME WRITE THE FIRST HEADLINE.

DON'T WE NEED A STORY?

FIRST THINGS FIRST.

"MR. SANDFLEET FIGHTING CANNIBALISTIC DESIRES."

STOP THE PRESSES!

38

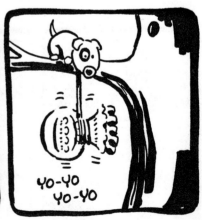

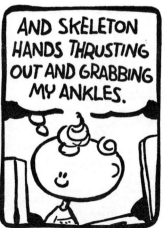

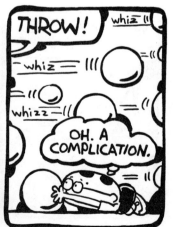

THERE'S ONE GOOD THING ABOUT NOVEMBER, HORTON. ...THANKSGIVING!

LOOK, SMEE, ALL YEAR THEY GIVE ME TURKEY HOT DOGS, TURKEY BALONEY, TURKEY MEATLOAF...

THANKSGIVING'S THE SAME STORY, ONLY MORE SO. SO WHAT'S THE BIG DEAL?

FAMILY?

AGAIN, SAME STORY ONLY MORE SO.

SMEE, MAKE A WISH.

IF YOU WISH FOR SOMETHING FOR YOURSELF, GOD WILL PUNISH YOU FOR SELFISHNESS. BETTER WISH FOR SOMETHING FOR ME.

READY?

WAIT A MINUTE!

IT WAS WORTH A TRY.

I'LL WISH FOR SOMETHING FOR YOU, AND YOU WISH FOR SOMETHING FOR ME.

THEN WE'LL BOTH BE UNSELFISH AND ONE OF US WILL STILL GET SOMETHING.

OK.

I WISH YOUR HAIR WOULD CATCH FIRE.

I WISH YOU WERE KIDNAPPED BY THE FULLER BRUSH MAN.

Dear Santa,

I know you keep track of who's been bad or good.

The facts in my case speak for themselves.

But let me present the case for moral relativism.

WHAT'D YOU COME UP WITH THIS YEAR?

THERE'S A LITTLE DOOR AT THE BOTTOM OF OUR CHIMNEY DOWN HERE BY THE FURNACE.

SINCE WE DON'T HAVE A FIREPLACE, MAYBE SANTA WILL COME OUT HERE.

MAYBE I SHOULD PUT MILK AND COOKIES HERE.

...OR A BROOM AND A DUSTPAN TO CLEAN HIM OUT.

I DIDN'T THINK THAT, SANTA. I DIDN'T EVEN THINK IT.

CHRISTMAS TREE! CHRISTMAS TREE!

ORNAMENTS TO DRAG ALL OVER THE HOUSE!

YAWLP!

BLUE SPRUCE! BLUE SPRUCE!

Panel 1: HORTON, IF SANTA IS FAIR,

Panel 2: HOW COME YOU ALWAYS GET MORE AND BETTER STUFF THAN ME?

Panel 3: THINK CAREFULLY WHETHER YOU REALLY WANT ME TO ANSWER THAT.

TOLES

Panel 4: I WITHDRAW THE QUESTION.

Panel 5: DAD, SINCE WE DON'T HAVE A FIREPLACE, IS SANTA GOING TO END UP IN OUR FURNACE?

Panel 6: NO, AURORA, AT OUR HOUSE HE COMES DOWN THE RAIN GUTTER AND IN THROUGH THE DOOR.

TOLES

Panel 7: YOU EXPECT ME TO BELIEVE THAT?

Panel 8: YOU WOULDN'T LIE ABOUT SOMETHING LIKE SANTA CLAUS, WOULD YOU, DAD?

Panel 9: SMEE, ON CHRISTMAS NIGHT SANTA COMES.

Panel 10: HE COMES DOWN THE CHIMNEY WITH HIS BAG OF TOYS.

Panel 11: HE PUTS THE TOYS UNDER THE TREE...

TOLES

Panel 12: THEN HE PUTS YOU IN THE BAG AND TAKES YOU TO THE NORTH POLE. YOU MEAN HE RESCUES ME FROM YOU?

Twas two days after Christmas, with a needle-less tree,

Not a creature was stirring, not Sonny, not Smee.

The stockings were strewn by the chimney somewhere, In realization nothing else was in there.

Their eyes, how they twinkled! Their faces, how merry! How much was it like this? By this morning, not very.

When all of a sudden, there arose such a clatter, I sprang from my bed to see what was the matter.

CRASH

I stumbled o'er puzzles, toys, games and some blocks, to see Sonny and Smee fighting over a box.

MY HOUSE. MINE!

YOU WANT TO GET POUNDED?

68

THE ONLY PROBLEM WITH THIS SNOW FURNITURE IS IT'S KIND OF COLD.

THAT'S WHY I BROUGHT OUT THE HOT COCOA.

WHERE?

I PUT THEM RIGHT HERE ON THE TABLE.

MY PARENTS HAVE PUT AWAY EVERY SINGLE OBJECT I COULD PUT IN MY MOUTH.

THEY THINK.

ANOTHER WHOLE DAY AHEAD OF ME TO PROVE THEM WRONG.

HERE WE GO... WE'LL BEGIN WITH A SAMPLING OF UPHOLSTERY BUTTONS FOR THE APPETIZER...

THE BOOKS ALL TELL MY PARENTS HOW TO CHILDPROOF A HOUSE.

MOM HAS CRAWLED AROUND ON HANDS AND KNEES PICKING UP EVERY LAST LITTLE THING.

AH, BUT THE BOOKS NEVER COVER OLDER SISTERS, NATURAL ALLIES IN THIS.

TIMON! YOU SPIT OUT AURORA'S DOLL HOUSE FURNITURE RIGHT THIS MINUTE!

IF THE PROFESSOR CAN MAKE A RADIO OUT OF COCONUT SHELLS...

...WHY DOESN'T HE JUST FIX THE HOLE IN THE BOAT?

THREE YEARS OF WATCHING "GILLIGAN'S ISLAND" RERUNS AND A SYNAPSE IN SMEE'S BRAIN UNEXPECTEDLY FIRES.

SMEE, DID YOU KNOW THAT THE SKIPPER AND MARY ANN ARE REALLY THE SAME PERSON?

YOU NOTICE HOW THEY NEVER APPEAR ON SCREEN TOGETHER?

...here on Gilligan's isle ♪

HE SAID THAT JUST AS THE SHOW WAS ENDING ON PURPOSE.

RASCAL, WHAT DO YOU DREAM ABOUT?

I DREAM ABOUT CHASING A BIG RABBIT.

REALLY?

I DREAM ABOUT A BIG RABBIT CHASING ME.

LOOK AT SMEE!

HE'S CHARGING THE ENEMY!

BRAVING A FLURRY OF SNOWBALLS! GOING RIGHT UP TO THE LEADER OF THE PIERCE ST. KIDS!

HE'S... HE'S... HE'S ASKING FOR HIS MITTEN BACK. IT EVIDENTLY STUCK TO HIS SNOWBALL.

ACTUALLY, GARDY AND VIOLET ARE HOLDING UP OUR END OF THE SNOWBALL FIGHT PRETTY WELL.

I GUESS YOU LEARN SOMETHING ABOUT PEOPLE IN COMBAT.

...LIKE WHO YOU'D WANT TO BE IN A FOXHOLE WITH.

HORTON. HE HAS THE SNACKS.

THE BEST TACTIC IN A SNOWBALL WAR IS GOOD POSITIONING.

SURPRISE THE ENEMY.

BE WHERE HE LEAST EXPECTS YOU TO BE.

THEY'LL NEVER FIND ME IN HERE.

NOBODY WANTS TO SUBSCRIBE TO THE CURIOUS OBSERVER, SONNY.

THEN WE'LL JUST HAVE TO DEPEND ON SINGLE COPY SALES, SMEE.

WHAT DOES THAT MEAN?

Dear "Editor",
A recent story in your "paper" said my husband, Amos Sandfleet, had cannibalistic tendencies.

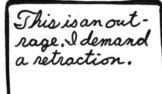

This is an outrage. I demand a retraction.

HORTON YOU HANDLE THIS.

Mrs. Sandfleet Eaten! Mr. Sandfleet Creates Raving Double in Laboratory As Replacement!

Dear Horton Lovejoy, "Cry Me a River" advice column:

I'm depressed about an upcoming birthday. Should I be?

CHEEZ KNEEZ

Think of it this way. Today is the last day of the first part of your life. You decide.

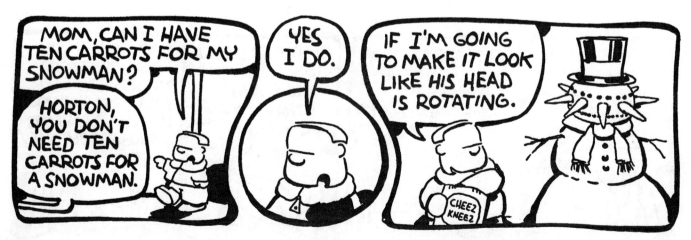

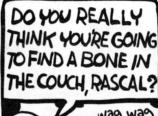

AURORA, WHAT ARE YOU DOING UP?

inch inch

I CAN'T SLEEP. CAN I GET IN MY SLEEPING BAG?

YES. JUST STAY IN IT.

inch inch

SONNY, DID YOU EVER DREAM YOU HAD A STAINLESS STEEL DRAIN IN YOUR LEG?

...AND ANTS WERE CRAWLING IN AND OUT OF IT?

NO, SMEE. THAT'S REALLY SICK. WHY, DID YOU?

UH, NO.

DAD, YOU KNOW WHAT I'D LIKE FOR MY ROOM?

A BUBBLING STREAM. WHAT DO YOU THINK?

I THINK IT WOULD LEAK THROUGH THE CEILING INTO THE LIVING ROOM.

A WATERFALL? YEAH! AND WE CAN HAVE A FISH LADDER ON THE STAIRS!

 THE BEST PART OF A SLEEPOVER IS SNEAKING OUTSIDE WITH FLASHLIGHTS.

 FREEDOM! EXCITEMENT! THE QUEST FOR ADVENTURE.

 RIGHT, SONNY? RIGHT? WHERE'D YOU GO?

 IT'S AN ADVENTURE STORY, HONEST, HORTON.

 DO YOU LIKE SLEEPING OVER, SONNY? SURE, HORTON. CHEE KNEE

 SLEEPING IN A STRANGE PLACE... THE EXPERIENCE OF AN UNFAMILIAR FLOOR?

 UM, YEAH, I GUESS.

 I DON'T SEE IT MYSELF. I'LL BE IN MY BED. 'NIGHT.

 IT'S BAD ENOUGH TRYING TO SLEEP ON HORTON'S FLOOR.

 ...IN MY CLOTHES BECAUSE I'M EMBARRASSED TO WEAR MY COWBOY PAJAMAS OVER HERE.

 BUT WORST OF ALL IS I KNOW THAT WHEN I... FINALLY... DO... START.... DROPPING .....OFF.......

 SONNY? ARE YOU ASLEEP YET? HORTON, DID I MENTION THAT I MURDER IN MY SLEEP? YEAH.

SONNY, WHERE IS YOUR REPORT? IT'S THE ONLY ONE STILL OUT.

I HAD IT, MISS BROWNING, I MUST HAVE LOST IT.

IT WAS ABOUT THE DEBASEMENT OF THE ANCIENT ROMAN MONETARY SYSTEM.

FUNNY, THAT'S WHAT HORTON'S REPORT IS ABOUT. YOU WEREN'T PLANNING TO COPY, WERE YOU?

HORTON!

HORTON, I CAN'T BELIEVE YOU STOLE MY SCHOOL REPORT.

AND WHY DID YOU TELL ME THAT STORY ABOUT HOW YOU WERE GOING TO JAM THE SCHOOL DOOR LOCK?

I WAS SO UPSET ABOUT THAT I...I...

...LOST TRACK OF YOUR REPORT?

OH DIABOLICAL, HORTON.

I SHOULD NEVER SPEAK TO YOU AGAIN, HORTON.

STEALING MY SCHOOL REPORT! I'M YOUR FRIEND.

RELAX, SONNY. I BOUGHT YOU A BIG BOX OF FRESH DONUTS.

HAVE I SOLD MY PRINCIPLES HERE? DID I GET A FAIR PRICE?

SONNY, SMEE, WE'RE INVITED TO UNCLE DUDLEY'S HOUSE FOR DINNER.

HE'S A VERY, WELL, PROPER GENTLEMAN, SO BEST BEHAVIOR PLEASE.

WHAT DOES THAT MEAN?

NO AUDIBLE GAGGING ON THE WEIRD FOOD DURING HIS ENDLESS DINNER MONOLOGUES.

UNCLE DUDLEY, DO YOU HAVE ANY...UM... TOYS? OTHER THAN AUNT ADDIE'S DOLLS, THAT IS.

WELL, SMEE...I'VE GOT A FASCINATING AUTOGRAPH COLLECTION YOU COULD LOOK AT.

YEAH?

19TH CENTURY GERMAN STATESMEN!

ANY YOU'D LIKE TO SEE? THERE'S A LONG STORY WITH EACH ONE.

I BET.

SMEE WON'T EAT VEGETABLES. I, HOWEVER, LOVE VEGETABLES.

Smirk

OH THEN YOU'LL LOVE AUNT ADDIE'S TURNIP-SPINACH MUSHROOM PASTE.

Smirk

Splatt

SMEE, THE CURIOUS OBSERVER IS DELAYERING.

WE'RE DOING SOME EXCESSING.

WE'RE DOWNSIZING.

WHAT?

NOBODY IS READING OUR PAPER.

NO WONDER.

YOU'RE FIRED! YOU DIDN'T SELL A SINGLE SUBSCRIPTION!

YOU DIDN'T EVEN SELL A SINGLE ISSUE!

I SOLD ONE TO MOM.

AND SHE SENT ME TO MY ROOM FOR MY EDITORIAL ON MRS. MILLER'S NEW HAIRSTYLE.

VIOLET, YOU'RE FIRED.

WE'RE DROPPING YOUR HOROSCOPE COLUMN. NOBODY READS IT.

EVERYBODY READS IT.

I GOT UP THIS MORNING THINKING, "TODAY IS A DAY FOR DECISIONS. ACT ON THEM."

I WROTE THAT.

TIMON, DO YOU TAKE THIS WOMAN, ME, TO BE YOUR LAWFULLY WEDDED WIFE?

WELL?

SILENCE RENDERS CONSENT.

AND ABSENCE MAKES THE HEART GROW FONDER!

I NOW PRONOUNCE US MAN AND WIFE.

NOW I THROW THE RICE ON US.

HONEY, YOU'RE NOT SUPPOSED TO EAT THE RICE!

GEE, THE NAGGING STARTS RIGHT AWAY.

TIMON, I'LL GIVE YOU A PENNY IF YOU GIVE ME ALL YOUR TOYS.

WOW! IF ONLY I ACTUALLY WANTED HIS TOYS.

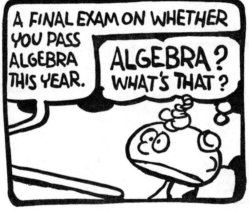